Papua New Guinea phrasebook

John Hunter

Papua New Guinea Phrasebook

Published by
    Lonely Planet Publications
    Head Office: PO Box 88, South Yarra, Victoria 3141, Australia
    Also: PO Box 2001A, Berkeley, CA 94702, USA

Printed by
    Colorcraft, Hong Kong

Illustrations
    Fiona Boyes

First published
    November 1986

National Library of Australia Cataloguing in Publication Data

Hunter, John.
    Papua New Guinea phrasebook

    ISBN 0 908086 90 3

    1. Pidgin English – Papua New Guinea – Conversation and phrase
    books – English. 1. Title (Series: Language survival kit).

427'.9953

©Lonely Planet, 1986

Contents

Introduction

There is no doubt that Neo-Melanesian, Melanesian Pidgin, or Pidgin as it is commonly called, has become an established language in Papua New Guinea. During the years of Australia's colonial rule over the country, which ended in 1975, Pidgin was often considered a childish, barbaric dialect of English. It was often referred to as 'Pidgin English'. Few of the colonial rulers saw it as more than a dialect of English and a temporary means of communication until Papua New Guineans learnt 'proper' English. There was even resistance to the translation of the Bible into Pidgin.

Today this is not the case. Pidgin is well established. It is a distinct living language with its own grammatical structure and vocabulary. It is now a first language among many Papua New Guineans, even replacing village languages. It is used in Parliament, on radio stations, in newspapers, and spoken by over one million inhabitants, *ja lingua franca*. It is spoken on the mainland and adjacent islands of Papua New Guinea, the Admiralty Islands, New Ireland, New Britain, the Solomon Islands, Vanuatu (with some variations), and parts of Irian Jaya (especially near the border).

In a country where there are in excess of 700 languages, the emergence of a 'lingua franca' is a necessity for national development. In Papua New Guinea, English, Hiri Motu and Pidgin have filled this role. Whilst English is still the language of instruction in schools, and the language of business, Pidgin is the language which a Papua New Guinean will speak in the village and/or outside the work place.

Like any language Pidgin is constantly changing. Those familiar with Pidgin twenty years ago will see many familiar pidgin words replaced with English words. This trend is unfortunately increasing. Despite the fact that Pidgin does contain many English words however, the best approach is to learn it as if it is a completely foreign language. Nearly all the words derived from English have changed their meanings: for example, *slip* from 'sleep' means 'lie down' or 'lying'.

Visitors to Papua New Guinea will find Pidgin invaluable when they move away from towns and talk with Papua New Guineans socially. Pidgin is an easy language to learn and once you've learnt a few phrases and words it is not difficult to both understand and make yourself understood. It will win you friends and break down communication barriers.

Pronunciation

Despite the fact that English is a major contributor to Pidgin vocabulary, the English promounciation is, at best, approximate. There are also some regional variations in pronunciation.

Vowels

Whilst English has 11 vowel sounds Pidgin has six.

a	as in 'art', for example:	*papa*	father
		man	man
		saksak	sago
e	as in 'bet', for example:	*beten*	prayer
		kek	cake
		ken	can
i	as in 'sit', for example:	*liklik*	little
		mi	me
		pikinini	child
i	as in 'machine', for example:	*lip*	leaf
		tripela	three
		hip	pile
o	as in 'pot', for example:	*dok*	dog
		toktok	talk
		sori	sorry
u	as in 'put', for example:	*lukluk*	appearance
		susu	milk
		suga	sugar

Pidgin speakers omit the off glides from vowels which are used in English, for example, name is pronounced 'nem' not 'neim'; go is 'go' and not 'gou'.

Dipthongs

There are only three dipthongs in Pidgin: ai, au, and oi.

ai	as in 'sign', for example:	*taim*	time
		insait	inside
		traim	to try
au	as in 'south', for example:	*nau*	now
		rausim	to remove
		kaukau	sweet potato
oi	as in 'soil', for example:	*boi*	boy
		boil	to boil

Consonants

Most consonants are pronounced as they are in English. The only area of difference concerns 'f' and 'p'. Words using the 'f' sound are rare, and many words sound the 'p' between 'f' and 'p', for example:

fire	*fire*
friend	*pren*
fight	*pait*

Stress

Most words are stressed on their first syllable.

Regional Variation

As you travel to different areas of Papua New Guinea, you will often encounter variations in the way Pidgin is spoken. The people of Manus Province claim their Pidgin is the purest form with fewer English words used and pure pronunciation.

Be that as it may, many Papua New Guineans have difficulty pronouncing groups of consonants especially at the beginning of words. Words beginning with st, sp, sk, pr, br, fr, tr, dr, kr, gr, pl, bl, fl, kl, and gl will sometimes be altered. Often, in order to say a word beginning like this, an extra vowel will be inserted between the consonants: *slek* (to be loose) can sound like 'silap' or 'salak', *plak* (flag) like 'pilak'. Spelling may also vary accordingly although this is neither correct nor recommended.

Grammar

All languages have a definite grammatical structure and
Pidgin is no exception. In this section you will find a few
general grammar rules which may or may not be passed over.
This chapter is not comprehensive and is not essential for
simple communication. More emphasis has been placed on
providing an extensive vocabulary so that the traveller will
have a wide list of words to use.

Articles

The definite article 'the' does not exist. The indefinite articles
'a' and 'an' are rendered by *wanpela*, or nothing at all.

I didn't see a man.
> *Mi no lukim wanpela man.*
> or
> *Mi no lukim man.*

Ol is used before a noun to indicate the plural. *Ol man* means
all the men being spoken about, not to be confused with
Olaman, an exclamation of surprise.

Nouns

Nouns have neither endings nor gender. Their context
indicates number and gender. Gender depends on the
presence or absence of adjectives; *man* means male and *meri*
means female, so a *dok meri* is a female dog. The distinction
between singular and plural is made with the use of
articles:

the man, this man, that man	*dispela man*
a man	*wanpela man*
the men, men	*ol man*
some men	*sampela man*
all men, all the men	*olgeta man*

Pidgin commonly compounds nouns whose first half consists of an attribute which restricts the meaning of the second half:

pupil	*skulboi*

Personal Pronouns

I, me	*mi*
you	*yu*
he, she, it, him, her, it	*em*
it (only as an object in a sentence)	*en*
we, us (excluding the person spoken to)	*mipela*
we, us (including the person spoken to)	*yumi*
you (plural)	*yupela*
they, them	*ol*

Numerals (*tu, tri*) are frequently incorporated in the plural pronouns:

the two of us, you and I	*yumitupela*
the two of us	*mitupela*
the three of us	*yumitripela*
the three of you	*yutripela*

Posession is indicated by placing *bilong* before the pronoun:

yours	*bilong yu*

Interrogative Pronouns

There are four members of this class of pronoun:

who and whom	*husat*
whose	*bilong husat*
what	*wanem*
which	*husat* or *wanem* depending on whether it is refering to a person or a thing respectively

Adjectives

Monosyllabic adjectives precede the noun, with ... *pela* attached:

big man	*bikpela man*
pretty woman	*naispela meri*

Adjectives with two or more syllables, or adjectival phrases, follow the noun:

bad man	*man nogut*
high mountain	*maunten i antap tumas*

The comparative is rendered by following the adjective with such particles as *moa* (more/very), *tru* (very), *tumas* (very much), *olgeta* (the ultimate/all/every), or by using the verb *win* (to surpass):

very big	*bikpela moa*
he is better than I	*em i win long me*

Verbs

Verbs are simply conjugated and undergo a minimum of changes. Context and inflection distinguish between the tenses. There is no passive voice and past participles are rendered as adjectives.

When the verb ends in *im* it is transitive:
  I know how to write a letter.
    Mi save raitim pas.

Pinis is added to a verb, or *bin* is placed before it, to form the past tense:
  I have gone.
    Mi go pinis.
    or
    Mi bin go.

Baimbai or *bai* are placed before a verb to form the future:
  I will go.
    Baimbai mi go.
    or
    Bai mi go.

In the third person singular and plural the verb is preceded by the predicate marker *i*. The first person plural and the second person plural forms after personal pronouns also usually have the predicate marker *i*:
  he goes (3rd person singular)
    em i go
  they go (3rd person singular)
    ol i go

We are well. (1st person plural)
Mipela i stap gut.
Where are you going? (1st person plural)
Yupela i go we?

Adverbs

Almost any adjective may be used as an adverb without change of form, however, adverbs never have the suffix -*pela*. Like adjectives, adverbs have the comparative particle *moa* (more) followed by either *olsem* (thus) or *long* (in/on/to/from etc). The superlative may also use *moa* (more), *tru* (very), *tumas* (very much), or *olgeta* (the ultimate/all/every) after the adverb:

He is closer than I am.
Em i stap moa klostu long mi.

Questions

How many, how much?	*Hamas?*
Where?	*We?*
What time?	*Wanem taim?*
Why?	*Bilong wanem?*
How?	*Olsem wanem?*
Who?	*Husat?*
What?	*Wanem samting?*

Many Pidgin statements can be made into questions which elicit 'yes' or 'no' by changing the pitch of the intonation so that it is higher than that for a statement and ends with a slight rise. Often the addition of *a* at the end of a statement will have the same effect:

Is your brother here?
> *Brata bilong yu i stap?*
> or
> *Brata bilong yu i stap, a?*

If you make a question in the negative, the answer will usually be different to what you would expect in English:

You didn't see him?	*Yu no lukim em?*
Yes I didn't.	*Yes.*
Did you see him?	*Yu lukem em, a?*
Yes I did.	*Yes.*

The word for 'yes' is *yes* and the word for 'no' is *nogat. No* in Pidgin means 'not':

No, I haven't got any money.
> *Nogat, mi no gat moni.*

Prepositions

There are basically two prepositions: *bilong* and *long*. *Bilong* may indicate possession, purpose or a characteristic trait:

(This is) my house.	*Haus bilong mi.*
(This is) good to eat.	*Gutpela kaikai.*
(He is) a pugnacious man.	*Man bilong pait.*

Long is used for all other prepositions, either alone or in conjunction with adverbs:

I am at the store.	*Mi stap long stoa.*

Conjunctions

and	*na*	man and woman	*man na meri*
or	*o*	big or little	*bikpela o liklik*
if	*sapos*	if you go	*sapos yu go*
but	*tasol*	but I did not go	*tasol mi no bin go*
when	*taim*	when you went	*taim yu go pinis*
			or
			taim yu bin go

Imperatives

Imperatives use plain sentence structures with *yu, yupela,* or *yumi, yumipela:*

You go (singular)	*Yu go*
You go (plural)	*Yupela go*
Let's go (you and I)	*Yumi go*
Let's go (if more than two)	*Yumipela go*

Pitfalls

Pilai can have three meanings. It could mean a game, fun or entertainment, or it could mean to play or have a game.

However, whenever it is used concerning adults or animals of different sexes it always means to have sexual intercourse.

Kilim means to beat or strike hard, not kill. To kill someone is *kilim i dai pinis*. *Kilim i dai* means to hit him hard enough to knock him out or make him sick; to *dai pinis* is to die-finish.

Greetings & Civilities

As you travel around Papua New Guinea you will be impressed with the friendliness and outgoing nature of the people. Unlike Western countries, people in Papua New Guinea will want to greet you and talk with you, whether you are known to them or not. This does not apply as much to women as, by tradition, most Papua New Guinean women will not speak to strangers.

Hello	*Gude*
Good morning	*Moning*
Good afternoon	*Apinun*
How are you?	*Yu stap gut?*
I am fine	*Mi stap gut*
Please	*Plis*
Excuse me	*Sori*
Thank you	*Tenkyu*
Goodbye	*Gutbai*, or *lukim yu*
See you later	*Lukim you bihain*
See you tomorrow	*Bai mi lukim yu tumora*

Forms of Address

Man	*Man*
Woman	*Meri*
Boy	*Boi* – it is derogatory to call men *boi* as this was the colonial term for all PNG males

18

Boy or schoolboy	*Manki*
Girl	*Liklik Meri*
Schoolchild of either sex	*Sumatin*
Older person of either sex	*Lapun* – age is traditionally respected

The terms *masta* and *misus* were colonial terms for European men and women. Like calling an adult *boi* it is better not to use these words as they imply an offensive attitude of European superiority. *Masta* and *misus* are still used in more remote areas.

Small Talk

As you travel around Papua New Guinea you may want to tell people about yourself. You will almost certainly be asked questions about yourself and the members of your family.

Meeting People

What language do you understand?
> *Tok ples bilong yu wanem?*

Do you speak English/Pidgin?
> *Yu save tok Inglis/Pisin?*

I speak ...
> *Mi save tok ...*

I don't understand.
> *Mi no save* or *Mi no klia gut.*

May I introduce you ...
> *Mi laik bai yu bungim ...*

I am pleased to meet you.
> *Mi hamamas long mitim yu.*

What is your name?
> *Wanem nem bilong yu?*

My name is John.
> *Nem bilong mi Jon.*

Where do you come from?	*Ples bilong yu we?*
	or
	Yu bilong wanem hap?
I am from ...	*Ples bilong mi ...*
Australia	*Ostrelya*
America	*Amerika*

Britain	*Englan*
New Zealand	*Niu Silan*
Canada	*Kanada*
Europe	*Yurop*
Germany	*Jermani*
Holland	*Holan*
Africa	*Aprika*

What is your job?	*Wanim kain wok bilong yu?*
I am a ...	*Mi ...*
teacher	*tisa*
doctor	*dokta*
clerk	*kuskus*
mechanic	*mekanik*
farmer	*man i wokim gaden*
fisherman	*man i hukim pis*
shopkeeper	*stoaman*
nurse	*nes* or *nes long haus sik*
student	*sumatin*
builder	*kapenta*
policeman	*polisman*
government worker	*wok wantaim gavman*

I don't have a job.	*Mi no got wok.*

Some useful phrases
May I take a photo?
  Inap mi kisim poto?
Are you married?
  Yu marit pinis? or *Yu marit o?*
Do you have children?
  Yu gat pikinini?

How old are you?
Hamas krismas bilong yu?
I am sorry.
Mi sori.
I am glad.
Mi hamamas tru.
I shall give you this.
Mi laik givim dispela samting long yu.
This is very nice.
Em i nais tumas.
That is bad.
Em i nogut.
I have enjoyed myself very much.
Mi hamamas tru.

The Family & Friends

Papua New Guinean family relationships can be very confusing to an outsider. If someone introduces you to his father (*papa*), he may not mean his paternal father but his father's brother. If you want to know if a relationship is a direct nuclear-family relationship as Europeans understand it you will need to ask if the *papa* is *papa tru*, or in the case of a person's mother, *mama tru*.

If a person is asked the names of relatives, including in-laws, they will most probably call them *papa*, *susa*, *tambu* (for example), or even a totally fictional name, in order to avoid using the real name which is believed to be magic.

Mother	*Mama* – may apply to a person's mother and all the mother's sisters
Father	*Papa* – may apply to a person's father and all the father's brothers

Brother	*Brata* – may also mean cousin, distant relative or friend
Sister	*Susa* – may also mean cousin distant relative or friend
Cousin	*Brata/Susa* – may also describe distant relatives or friends
Child (boy)	*Pikanini man*
Child (girl)	*Pikanini meri*
Husband	*Man bilong mi/em/yu*
Wife	*Meri bilong mi/em/yu*
Sister/brother-in-law	*Tambu*
Grandmother/father	*Tumbuna*
Friend	*Pren, Brata, Susa, Poroman*

The word *wantok* is frequently used to describe someone who speaks the same language, is of the same nationality, is a neighbour, has something in common with you, or is a friend.

Feelings

I feel hot.	*Mi hat.*
I feel cold.	*Mi kol.*
I feel happy.	*Mi amamas.*
I am sad.	*Bel bilong mi nogut.*
I feel tired.	*Mi les* or *skin i les.*
I feel hungry.	*Mi hangre.*
I feel filled.	*Mi pulap.*
I am thirsty.	*Nek bilong mi drai.*
I feel drunk.	*Mi spak.*
I feel scared.	*Mi pret.*
I feel angry.	*Mi kros* or *bel i hat.*
I like you (very much).	*Mi laikim yu (tru).*

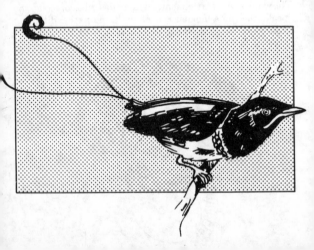

Animals

ants	*anis*
bull/cow	*bulmakau*
cassowary	*muruk*
cat	*pusi*
crocodile	*pukpuk*
cuscus	*kapul*
dog	*dok*
insect	*binatang*
mosquito	*natnat*
pig	*pik*
sheep	*sipsip*
snake	*snek*
bird	*pisin*
Bird of Paradise	*kumul*

Plants

tree	*diwai*
grass	*gras*
flower	*plaua* or *pur pur*

Accommodation

Accommodation in Papua New Guinea is generally expensive. Some towns have lodges which are more basic than hotels and cheaper. There are no hostels and you should seek permission before camping.

Where is the ...?	*I stapwe ...?*
hotel	*hotel*
house	*haus*
church	*haus lotu*
(village) chief	*luluai*

Please take me to the hotel.
Plis kisim mi i go long hotel.
How far is it?
Em i longwe o nogat?
Is this the hotel?
Em dispela hotel?
Is there somewhere I can sleep in the village tonight?
Inup mi slip long ples long nait?
How much will it cost?
Kostim hamas?
I will pay ... kina, OK?
... kina inup o nogat?

At the Hotel

Do you have ...?	Yu gat ...?
a room	rum
a bedroom	rum slip
a bed	bet
a blanket	blanket
a bathroom	rum waswas
a curtain	laplap bilong windo
a dining room	rum kaikai
a light	lait
a mirror	glas bilong lukluk

I want a room with ....
  Mi laikim rum i gat ....
I want to see the room now.
  Mi laik lukim rum nau.
Have you got a single/double room?
  Yu gat rum i got wanpela/tupela bet?

Where is the toilet?
Haus pekpek i stap we?
How much is the room and food?
Rum na kaikai i hamas?
I like this room.
Mi laikim dispela rum
I like that room.
Mi laikim dispela (narapela) rum long hap.
I want to see another room.
Mi laik lukim narapela rum.

I want to stay . . . .   *Mi laik stap long . . . .*
    one day   *wanpela de*
    one week   *wanpela wik*

Could I have the key of my room please?
Mi laikim ki bilong rum bilong mi, plis?
Are there any letters for me/us?
Yu gat sampela pas i kam long mi/mipela o nogat?
Could I speak to . . . please?
Mi laik toktok wantaim long . . . plis?
It has to do with . . . .
Em i toktok long . . . .
It is very important.
Em i bikpela samting tumas or *Em i bikpela tok tok.*

I would like a bath.
Mi laik waswas.
I need some soap/a towel/hotwater.
Mi laikim sop/taul/hatwara.

Is the restaurant open/closed?
  Haus kaikai i op/pas?
Could I see the menu?
  Mi laik lukim pas bilong ol kaikai?
I would like . . . .
  Mi laik . . . .
Waiter, the bill please.
  Yu bringim bil, plis or *Karim i kam pas bilong hamus.*

Would you take my luggage to the bus please?
  Yu karim i go ol bek bilong mi long bas, plis?
There is just one bag.
  Mi gat wanpela bek tasol.
There are two bags and a bundle.
  Mi gat tupela bek na dispela karamap.

Getting Around

There are all sorts of ways of travelling around Papua New Guinea. The rugged nature of the country makes travelling long distances often only possible by plane. Where there are road links, which occur on the north side of the Owen Stanley Ranges, the cheapest form of travel is by PMV (Public Motor Vehicle). PMVs are usually 15 to 20 seater buses. There is usually a set fare over the route to be travelled. Boats travel from towns to the outlying islands.

People in Papua New Guinea are very friendly and will go out of their way to help. A traveller must be careful that he does not intrude or over use hospitality since a Papua New Guinean will not complain about a person's demands. A payment or gift should be given for services rendered. Never accept a gift unless you are prepared to give something in return.

Visitors should dress modestly and behave carefully. It is only polite to ask if you may take a photo of someone. There are also taboos (*tambu*) which should be observed. If in doubt ask. For example, in the Southern Highlands it is wrong for a man to step over a women's possessions and wrong for women to enter certain houses.

Where is . . .?	. . . *i stap we?*
the ticket office	*Tiket opis*
the boat	*Bot*
the taxi	*Teksi*
the aircraft	*Balus*
the airport	*Ples balus*

the car	*Ka*
the road	*Rot*
the island	*Ailin*
the bus	*Bas*
the bus stop	*Bas stop*
the PMV	*PMV*

Show me please.
Soim mi plis.

Please call a taxi for me.
Singaut long teksi i kam long mi.

Where does the bus go?
Bas i go we?

Do you go to ...?
Yu go long ...?

What time does the bus go?
Bas i go wanem taim?

The bus is late.
Bas i bihain taim.

The bus has already gone.
Bas i go pinis.

The bus is going to the town.
Bas i go long taun.

The bus is going to the bush.
Bas i go long bus.

What time are you going?
Wanem taim bai yu go?

What time are you returning?
Wanem taim bai yu kambek gen?

I am arriving today/tomorrow.
Bai mi kam tude/tumora.

I am going today/tomorrow.
Bai mi go tude/tumora.
I am returning today/tomorrow.
Bai mi kambek gen tude/tumora.
I want to buy a ticket.
Mi laik baim pas bilong balus/PMV.

Directions

A Papua New Guinean's idea of distance is frequently different to a European's. You may be told a village is quite near (*klostu liklik*), only to find it is many hours further on, or that a river is just over the next hill, which could also mean a very long way.

fairly near	*klostu liklik*
distant	*longwe*
fairly distant	*longwe liklik*
very distant	*longwe tumas*
go	*go*
north	*not*
south	*saut*
east	*is*
west	*wes*
on the opposite side	*long hapsait*
there	*long hap*
up	*antap*
down	*daun*
turn left/right	*tanim lep/rait*
straight ahead	*stret*
inside	*insait*
outside	*ausait*

Bushwalking

One of the least known of Papua New Guinea's attractions is the opportunity it offers for mountaineering and bushwalking in the high interior ranges, one of the most beautiful and exotic settings in the world. Adventuring in Papua New Guinea, however, isn't for the novice and requires more care and preparation than for many other places.

Lonely Planet's guide *Bushwalking in Papua New Guinea* has comprehensive information, route descriptions for a number of spectacular walks, and a language section for Hiri Motu a language still commonly used in the former Papuan provinces.

If local guides are required, advance notice should be given to local officials or missionaries. A guide (who will probably speak Pidgin) is essential for many of the treks as tracks may be difficult to follow, permission is needed to travel through some areas, communication needs to be made with local tribes, and local information needs to be gathered regarding food and accomodation. Rates of pay for guides and carriers usually involve bargaining.

There are no designated camping areas in Papua New Guinea except for the Baiyer River Bird Sanctuary, nor is it safe or possible to camp in towns. In villages or isolated areas, tents may be pitched, but permission to do this must be gained from the local land owner. This must be done no matter how isolated the area might appear.

Hiring

Excuse me, can you help?
> *Plis yu nap halpim?*

We need three porters and a guide to help us.
> *Mipela laik tripela kagoboi na wanpela gait. (Kagoboi is the name of the job and is not derogatory.)*

Is the guide experienced in this region?
> *Gait, i save dispela ples o nogat?*

We are going to ....
> *Yumi go long ....* (includes person spoken to)
> *Mipela go long ....* (excludes person spoken to)

The porters will only be required for two days.
> *Mi laik kagoboi long tupela de tasol.*

We'd like one man to guide us to the top.
> *Mipela laik wanpela man soim rot i go antap.*

The porters will be paid four kina a day.
> *Mipela peim kagoboi fopela kina long wanpela wanpela de.*

Including food.
  Wantaim kaikai.
With/without a load.
  Wantaim kago/i no wantaim kago.
I want to buy a canoe.
  Mi laik baim kanu.
I want to hire a canoe for ... days.
  Mi laik baim kanu long ... pela de.
How much will it cost?
  Kostim hamas?

Accommodation

May we pitch our tents and stay here the night?
  Plis, mi laik putim haus sel long hia na stap long nait. I orait?
Where can we pitch our tents and stay the night?
  Bai mi putim haus sel long wanem hap?
Is there somewhere in the village we can sleep?
  I gat sampela hap long ples mipela inap slip?
How much will it cost?
  Kostim hamas?

Is ... available?   ... *i stap o nogat?*
    food   *Kaikai*
    water   *Wara*
    firewood   *Diwai bilong mekim paia*

Instructions

Would you fetch some water please?
  Plis, yu kisim wara?
Bring it here.
  Kisim i kam.

You are right.
Yu tok stret.
Wait here for our return.
Yu stap na wet inap mipela kam bek.
We will be back tomorrow night.
Bai mipela kam bek long tumora nait.
Take this urgently to the official at the airfield.
Plis, yu givim dispela samting long bos long ples balus kwiktaim.
Do it like this.
Mekim olsem long dispela.
We will rest here a little while.
Yumi stap liklik or *Yumi malolo lik lik.*
We will stay here tonight.
Yu mi stap hia long nait.
Please come over here.
Plis, yu kam.
I need to open that pack.
Mi laik opim karamap.
Where are you going?
Yu go we?
Where have you come from?
Yu kamap long wanem ples?
If we are not back here in five days, tell the government official at . . . .
Sapos mipela no kambek long faipela de bai yu tok long ol bos long dispel samting long . . . .

Directions

Where is the	. . . i stap we?
village	ples or
	bikpela man long ples

chief	*luluai*
trail	*rot*
resting place	*ples bilong malolo*
airfield	*ples balus*
government office	*ofis bilong gavman*
school	*skul*
mission	*stesin/misin*
river	*wara*
canoe	*kanu*

Which is the way to ...?
Wanem rot long ...?
Go straight ahead.
Go stret.
Turn right/left.
Tanim rait/lep.
Are there any tracks in the direction of ...?
I gat rot i go long ...?
Is this track still in use?
Dispela rot i orait or nogat.
How long will it take to get to ...?
Wanem taim bai yumi kamap long ...?
How far away is ...?
... i stap we?

What is the name of this ...?	*Wanem nem bilong dispela ...?*
village	*ples*
mountain	*maunten*
river	*wara*

Weather

The weather will be hot tomorrow.
Tumora bai i kamap hat.
The weather will be cold tomorrow.
Tumora bai i kamap kol.
Tomorrow will be sunny.
Tumora bai san i lait.
Tomorrow will be rainy.
Tumora bai ren i kamdaun.
Tomorrow will be cloudy.
Tumora bai klaut i pas.
Tomorrow will be windy.
Tumora bai win i kamap.

Worth Noting

Pidgin often adds *o nogat* (or not) to the end of a statement making it into a question that expects a 'yes' or 'no' answer, for example:

Will it rain tomorrow?
Tumora bai ren i kamdaun o nogat?

Around Town

This section has activities and services you may be interested in. Town life is in marked contrast to village life. Here, the traditional is replaced by the modern: electricity, restaurants, shops, sporting facilities, hotels, picture theatres, schools, cars .... English is commonly used in shops and official offices like post offices.

The main form of transport within towns is the PMV. These 15 seater buses have more or less set routes, especially in the larger towns. A passenger can usually get on or off anywhere along the route. The fare is paid as you leave and is usually very reasonable. Drivers are very helpful and will tell you when to get off or how to get to a certain place.

It is not advisable to walk around the towns at night by yourself. It is also necessary to make sure your belongings are locked safely away. Never leave bags unattended. Papua New Guinean towns have their share of crime, although the situation is not as bad as in many other countries. With care and sensible security there should not be any problems.

Where is the ...?	... i stap we?
bank	Haus mani
shop	Stoa
theatre	Haus piksa
hospital	Haus sik

I want to go to	Mi laik go long ....
the police station	polis stesin
the restaurant	haus kaikai

| the school | *skul* |
| the market | *maket* or *bung* |

At the Post Office

In Papua New Guinea there is no house delivered mail. Mail either has to be addressed to a Post Box or care of a Post Office. The mail service is very good with airmail to Australia taking less than a week.

The telephone service is as up-to-date as anywhere in the world. You can ring international numbers directly.

post office	*post opis*
surface mail	*surfismel*
air mail	*salim pas i go long balus*
registered mail	*rejistidmel*

I want to	*Mi laik ....*
send a letter	*salim pas*
write a letter	*raitim pas*
address a letter	*adresim pas*
answer a letter	*bekim pas*
weigh the letter	*skelim pas*
send a parcel	*salim karamap*
talk on the phone	*tok long telepon*
change my money	*senisim mani*

What time is the ... open?
Wanem taim ... i op?
I would like to make a telephone call.
Mi laik toktok long telepon.
Would you call ... for me?
Mi laik bai yu putim telipon long ....
There is no answer.
Telipon i ring tasol nogat ansa.
I have been cut off.
Swis i katim toktok bilong mitupela.
Could I have some notepaper/airmail paper/envelopes?
Plis mi laik sampela pepa bilong raitim pas/sampela emel pepa/sampela skin pas?
Where can I buy stamps?
Mi baim stem we?
How much altogether?
Olgeta hamas?

Forms

name	*nem bilong yu*
address	*atres bilong yu*
nationality	*as ples bilong yu*

age	*hamas krismas bilong yu*
date of birth	*de mama i karim yu*
occupation	*wanem kain wok bilong yu?*
signature	*raitim nem bilong yu*

At the Bank

The unit of currency in Papua New Guinea is the *Kina* (K). It is made up of 100 *toea* (t). Coins are 1t, 2t, 5t, 10t, 20t, 50t, and K1. Notes are K2, K5, K10, and K20. Most large towns have one or two banks.

bank	*haus mani*
money	*mani*
cheque/cheque book	*sek/sekbuk*
travellers' cheque	*travellers' cheque*

I want to	*Mi laik ....*
change money	*senisim mani*
deposit money	*putim mani long haus mani*
withdraw money	*rausim mani long haus mani*
cash a cheque	*senisem sek long mani*
What time is the bank open?	*Wanem taim haus mani i op?*

Emergencies

I need help.
   Mi laikim sampela halp.
I am in trouble.
   Mi gat trabel.

Please give this message to a policeman/doctor/ teacher.
Plis yu givim dispela tok long polisman/dokta/tisa.

Do it very fast.
Kwiktaim tru.

What do you want?
Yu laik wanem samting.

What is the matter?
Olsem wanem?

Don't you worry.
Yu no ken wori.

Speak slowly/softly.
Tok isi.

Speak loudly.
Tok strong.

Shout.
Singaut.

<u>INSTRUCTIONS FOR THE OPERATION OF THE EMERGENCY LOCATOR BEACON.</u>
Remove Rubber Plug, Insert Finger & Push The Rubber Toggle Switch Downwards.

<u>SAPOS BALUS I BUGARAP, YU MAS WORKIM DISPELA OL SAMTING.</u>
Rausim Lik Lik Gumi, Putim Finga Bilong Yu Long Hole Na Suim Switch Oli
Karamapim Long Gumi Igo Daun.

Workim Ol Dispela Samting Taim Balus I Bugarap.

Food

Some Useful Phrases

Is the restaurant open/closed?
Haus kaikai i op/pas?
I would like to see the menu.
Mi laik lukim pas bilong ol kaikai.
I don't want to eat. I will only have a drink
Mi no laik kaikai. Mi dring tasol.
Make coffee/tea.
Wokim copi/ti.
Pour milk into the coffee/tea.
Kapsaitim susu long copi/ti.
Share out the rice please.
Skelim rais plis.
I (would) like ....
Mi laik ....
I don't like ....
Mi no laik ....
I didn't ask for ....
Mi no askim long dispela ....
Please bring the bill.
Bringim pas bilong kostim kaikai.

Some Useful Words

food	*kaikai*
sandwiches	*sanwis*
dessert	*switkai*
salt	*sol*
pepper	*pepa*

sugar	*suga*
knife	*naip*
fork	*pork*
spoon	*spun*
glass	*glas*
plate	*plet*
breakfast	*kaikai bilong moningtem*
lunch	*kaikai long belo*
dinner	*kaikai long nait*
snack	*liklik kaikai*
hot	*hat*
fresh	*nupela*
stale	*nogut*
clean	*klin*
dirty	*doti*

Cooking

cook/to cook	*kuk/kukim*
fry/to fry	*prai/praim*
frying pan	*praipan*
boil/to boil	*boil/boilim*
saucepan	*sospen*
steam	*mumu*

Drinks

drink/to drink	*dring/dringim*
water	*wara*
ice	*ais*
alcohol	*spiris/wiski*
beer	*bia*
coffee	*copi*
tea	*ti*

milk	*susu*
lemonade, sweet drink	*loli wara*
Fill my glass.	*Pulapim glas bilong mi.*
Half fill my glass	*Pulapim hap tasol.*

Meat

meat	*abus*
chicken	*kakaruk*
pork	*pik*

Seafood

to fish with hook and line	*hukim*
saltwater	*solwara*
fish	*pis*
crayfish	*kindam*
octopus	*kurita*
crabs	*kuka*
shark	*sak*
squid	*tauka*

Fruit

banana	*banana*
ripe coconut	*kokonas*
green coconut	*kulau*
orange/lemon	*muli*
pineapple	*painup*
pawpaw	*popo*

Vegetables

sweet potato	*kaukau*
taro	*taro*
yam	*yam*

tapioca	*tapiok*
rice	*rais*
ginger	*kawawar*
sago	*saksak*
asparagus	*pitpit*
pandanus	*karuka marita*
breadfruit	*kapiak*
cucumber	*kukumba*
bean	*bin*
onion	*anian*
tomato	*tomato*

Shopping

In the towns and villages of Papua New Guinea there are fixed prices on goods. There is usually little room for bargaining except in the more remote areas.

I want to buy	*Mi laik baim ....*
How much is it?	*Hamas long em?*
How much is this?	*Dispela i hamas?*
I would like to buy this please.	*Mi laik baim dispela, plis.*
That is too dear.	*Em i dia tumas.*
I don't want this.	*Mi no laik.*

Clothing

shoes	*su*
coat	*kot*
cap	*hat*
pants	*trausis*
shirt	*siot*
skirt	*sket*
socks	*sokin*
bag	*bilum*

Toiletries & Accessories

scissors	*sisis*
thread	*tret*
comb	*kom*
razor	*resa*
soap	*sop*

| toothbrush | *bras bilong tit* |
| toothpaste | *sop bilong tit* |

Camera Supplies
camera	*kamera*
film	*pilum*
black and white	*blak na wait*
colour	*kala*
photograph	*piksa*
develop	*wasim*

Stationary
book	*buk*
ink	*ing*
pencil	*pensil*
paper	*pepa*
ruler	*rula*
pen	*pen*
newspaper	*niuspepa*
envelope	*skin pas*

Colours
colour	*kala*
white	*waitpela*
black	*blakpela*
red	*retpela*

Size & Comparison
small	*liklik*
smaller	*liklik moa*
smallest	*liklik long ol* or *liklik tumas*
strong	*strongpela*

stronger	*strongpela moa*
strongest	*strongpela long ol* or *strongpela tumas*
good	*gutpela*
very good	*gutpela moa*
excellent	*winim ol* or *gutpela tumas*
a lot	*planti*
a large amount	*planti moa*
a great deal	*planti tumas*
big	*bik*
very big	*bikpela moa*
huge	*bikpela tumas*
heavy	*hevi*
high	*antap*

Measures

gram	*giram*
kilogram	*kilogiram*
litre	*lita*
centimetre	*sentimita*
metre	*mita*
kilometre	*kilomita*

Health

Papua New Guinea is a tropical country and a visitor must take precautions against tropical illnesses. No vaccinations are required for entry if the visitor arrives from an area free from cholera and typhoid. Malaria tablets must be taken to guard against malaria which is very common.

I am ill.
  Mi gat sik.
Where can I see a doctor?
  Mi painim dokta we?
Please get a doctor.
  Plis, yu go tokim dokta, bai i kam.
Please send a message to ....
  Bai yu salim tok long ... plis.
Please carry me to ....
  Karim mi long ... plis.
Please give me ....
  Givim mi ... plis.
I would like some water.
  Mi laikim wara bilong dring.

Where is ...?	... i stap we?
the hospital	*Haus sik*
the doctor	*Dokta*
the dentist	*Dokta bilong tit*
the chemist	*Kemis*

I have	*Mi gat ....*
toothache	*pen long tit*
a sore	*sua ....*
stomach ache	*bel i pen*
head ache	*het i pen*
diarrhoea	*pekpek wara*
broken bone	*bun i bruk*
giddy	*ai i raun*
burn	*kukim skin*
a cold	*kus*
fever	*fiva*
sprain	*tanim skru bilong lek/han*

Parts of the Body

head	het
hair	gras
whiskers	mausgras
forehead	poret
ear	ia
eye	ai
nose	nus
mouth	maus
saliva	spet
teeth	tit
neck	nek
arm	han
hand	han
anus	as
faeces	pekpek
urine	pispis
leg	lek
foot	lek

At the Chemist

I want ....   *Mi laikim ....*
     medicine   *marasin*
     tablet   *tablet*
     adhesive plaster   *plasta*
     antiseptic   *marasin bilong klinim*
                                    soa

     aspirin   *asprin*
     bandage   *banis*
     doctor   *dokta*

Time

day	*de*
week	*wik*
month	*mun*
year	*yia*
day after tomorrow	*haptumora*
day before yesterday	*asde bipo*
yesterday	*asde*
tomorrow	*tumora*

Days of the Week

Monday	*Mande*
Tuesday	*Tunde*
Wednesday	*Trinde*
Thursday	*Fonde*
Friday	*Fraide*
Saturday	*Sarere*
Sunday	*Sande*

Months

January	*Janueri*
February	*Februeri*
March	*Mas*
April	*Epril*
May	*Me*
June	*Jun*
July	*Julai*
August	*Ogas*
September	*Septemba*

October	*Oktoba*
November	*Novemba*
December	*Decemba*

Some Useful Phrases

What time is it?	*Wanem taim nau?*
It is five o'clock.	*Emi i faiv kilok.*
It is ten past five.	*Emi i ten minut bihain long faiv kilok.*
It is ten to five.	*Ten minut i go bilong painim faiv kilok.*
What day is it?	*Wanem de?*

Numbers

The suffix *-pela* is added to the stem for counting objects. Numbers without *-pela* are used for prices, time and arithmetic.

1	*wan*
2	*tu*
3	*tri*
4	*foa*
5	*faiv*
6	*sikis*
7	*seven*
8	*et*
9	*nain*
10	*ten*

The numbers 11 – 19 are formed by adding the numbers *wan* to *nain* after *wanpela ten*

11	*wanpela ten wan*
12	*wanpela ten tu*
13	*wanpela ten tri*
14	*wanpela ten foa*
15	*wanpela ten faiv*
16	*wanpela ten sikis*
17	*wanpela ten seven*
18	*wanpela ten et*
19	*wanpela ten nain*

After 19 tens are formed by using the numbers *tu* onwards
with the ending *-pela*.

20	*tupela ten*
25	*tupela ten faiv*
30	*tripela ten*
35	*tripela ten faiv*
40	*fopela ten*
45	*fopela ten faiv*
50	*faivpela ten*
55	*faivpela ten faiv*
60	*sikispela ten*
65	*sikispela ten faiv*
70	*sevenpela ten*
75	*sevenpela ten faiv*
80	*etpela ten*
85	*etpela ten faiv*
90	*nainpela ten*
95	*nainpela ten faiv*
100	*wan handet*
101	*wan handet wan*
1,000	*tausen*
10,000	*tenpela tausen*
100,000	*handetpela tausen*
1,000,000	*wan milian*
once	*wanpela*
twice	*tupela*
thrice	*tripela*
four times	*foapela taim*

10 times	*tenpela taim*
11 times	*wanpela ten wan taim*
22 times	*tupela ten tu taim*
1/2	*hap*

Vocabulary

A

above – *antap long*
accident – *bagarap*
address – *adres*
adult – *bikpela man*
advertisement – *toksave*
aerogramme – *leta pas*
afraid – *pret*
after – *bihain long*
afternoon – *apinun*
again – *gen*
against – *i go long*
agree – *yesa*
air (n) – *win*
air conditioner – *win masin*
air mail – *mel long balus*
airplane – *balus*
airport – *ples balus*
alive – *i gat laip*
all – *olgeta*
all right – *orait*
almost – *klostu*
alone – *wanpela tasol*
already – *yet*
also – *tu*
although – *maski*
always – *oltaim*
among – *namel long*

and – *na*
angry – *kros*
animal – *abus*
another one (different) – *narakain*
another one (more) – *narapela*
answer – *bekim tok*
antiseptic – *marasin bilong klinim sua*
apartment – *rum*
approximately – *samting olsem*
arm (n) – *han*
army – *ami*
around – *nabaut*
arrive – *kamap*
art – *samting tumbuna*
art gallery – *haus tambaran*
artificial – *man i wokim*
ask – *askim*
at – *long*
attempt – *traim*
awake – *i no slip*

B

baby – *pikinini*
back (rear) – *baksait*
back (again) – *bek*
backwards – *long bek*
bad – *nogut*
bag (n) – *bek*
baggage – *kago*
ballpoint – *pen bolpoin*
bamboo shoots – *ol pikinini mambu*
banana – *banana*

bank (n) – *haus mani*
bathe – *waswas*
bathroom – *ples waswas*
battery – *bateri*
beach (n) – *nambis*
beans – *ol bin*
beard – *mausgras*
beautiful – *nais*
because – *bilong wanem*
because of – *long*
become – *kamap*
bed – *bet*
beef – *abus bulmakau*
beer – *bia*
before (time) – *bipo long taim*
behind – *bihain long*
believe – *bilipim*
bell – *belo*
best – *nambawan*
better – *mobeta*
beyond – *narasait long*
bicycle (n) – *wilwil*
big – *bikpela*
bill – *bil*
binoculars – *glas bilong kapten*
bird – *pisin*
biscuit – *biskit*
black – *blakpela*
blanket – *blanket*
blood – *blut*
blue – *blu*
boat – *bot*

body – *skin*
boiled – *i bin boilim*
book – *buk*
boot (n) – *bikpela su*
born – *mama i karim*
both – *tupela*
bottle – *botol*
bottle opener – *op tin*
bottom – *ananit*
box (n) – *bokis*
boy – *pikinini man*
bra – *banis bilong susu*
brake – *brek*
brave – *i no save pret*
bread – *bret*
break – *brukim*
breakfast – *kaikai long moning*
bridge (n) – *bris*
bring – *kisim … i kam*
brooch – *bros*
brown – *braun*
brush (n) – *brus*
bundle – *karamap*
bus – *bas*
businessman – *man bisnis*
busy – *i gat wok*
but – *tasol*
butter – *bata*
button – *baten*
buy – *baim*

C

cabbage – *kapis*
cake – *kek*
call (telephone) – *ring long telipon*
called, is – *nem bilong . . . i*
call out – *singaut*
camera – *kamera*
candle – *kandel*
captain (of ship) – *kapten*
car – *kar*
carefully – *isi isi*
cargo – *kago*
carpet – *mat* or *tepik*
carrot – *karot*
carry – *karim*
cat – *pusi*
centimetre – *sentimita*
century – *handet yia*
certainly – *orait orait*
chair – *sia*
change (small money) – *senis*
change money (from notes to coins) – *senisim*
change money (from one currency to another) – *tanim mani*
change (transport) – *senisim*
cheap – *i no dia*
cheese – *sis*
cherry – *sirsen*
chicken – *kakaruk*
chief – *luluai*
child – *pikinini*
chocolate – *braunpela loli*

choose – *kisim long laik*
chopsticks – *sopstik*
church – *haus lotu*
cigar – *siga*
cigarette – *sigaret*
cinema – *haus piksa*
city – *biktaun*
clean – *klin*
clean (vb) – *klinim*
clerk – *kuskus*
clock – *kilok*
close – *pasim*
closed – *i pas*
cloth – *laplap*
clothes – *klos*
coast (n) – *nambis*
coat – *kot*
coffee – *kopi*
coin – *mani ain*
cold – *kol*
cold season (winter) – *taim bilong kol*
colour (n) – *kala*
comb (n) – *kom*
come – *kam*
comfortable – *gut moa*
commercial – *bilong bisnis*
company (firm) – *kampani*
complain – *kotim*
completely – *olgeta*
conceal – *haitim*
concert – *singsing*
consul – *tultul*

contain – *holim ... i stap*
continue – *skruim ... i go*
convenient – *i mekim isi*
conversation – *toktok*
cook (vb) – *kukim*
cookie – *biskit*
corkscrew – *skru tuptup*
corner – *kona*
corridor – *ples wokabaut insait long haus*
costs – *kastim*
cotton – *katen*
cotton-wool – *kapuk*
count (vb) – *kaunim*
country (nation) – *kantri*
countryside – *bus*
courtyard – *kot*
cover (vb) – *karamapim*
crab – *kuka*
cream – *strongpela susu*
cross (vb) – *go long hap long*
crowd – *planti man na meri*
cup – *kap*
curry – *kari*
cushion – *pilo*
custom (way) – *pasin*
customs (n) – *kastam*
cut (vb) – *katim*

D

dance – *singsing* or *danis*
dangerous – *i gat samting nogut*
dark (colour) – *tudak*

dark (no light) – *tudak*
dates – *prut det*
day – *de*
daytime – *taim long san*
dead – *i dai pinis*
dear (expensive) – *dia*
decide – *pasim tingting*
deep – *godaun tru*
demand (vb) – *singaut long*
dentist – *dokta bilong tit*
desert (n) – *ples wesan*
diamond – *daimen*
dictionary – *buk bilong pairim mining*
die – *dai pinis*
different – *narapela kain*
difficult – *i hatwok*
dinner – *kaikai long belo*
direction – *i makim rot*
dirty – *doti*
do (vb) – *mekim*
doctor – *dokta*
dog – *dok*
don't! – *nogat!*
door – *dua*
doubt – *tubel*
down – *daun*
dress (woman's) – *klos meri*
drink (n) – *dring*
drink (vb) – *dringim*
drive (vb) – *draivim*
driver – *draiva*
dry – *drai*

duck (n) – *pato*
during – *long taim bilong*
dusty – *i gat dus*
duty (obligation) – *wok*

E

each – *wanpela wanpela*
each other – *wanpela narapela*
early (before time) – *bipotaim*
earrings – *ol bilas bilong ia*
east – *hap san i kamap* or *es*
easy – *isi*
eat – *kaikaim*
egg (n) – *kiau*
either/or – *ating*
electric – *lektrik*
elevator – *lipt*
embassy – *haus luluai bilong longwe ples*
empty – *nating* or *pinis*
enemy – *birua*
engine – *ensin*
enjoy – *hamamas tru*
enormous – *bikpela tru*
enough – *inap*
enter – *kam insait long*
entrance – *dua i kam insait*
envelope – *skin pas*
equal – *wankain*
evening – *apinun*
everybody – *olgeta man*
everything – *olgeta samting*
everywhere – *long olgeta ples*

exactly – *stret*
example, for – *wankain olsem*
except – *tasol i no gat*
exhibition – *so*
exit (n) – *dua i go ausait*
expect – *wetim*
expensive – *dia*
explain – *tok save long*
eye – *ai*

F

face – *pes olgeta*
fact, in – *em i tru*
fail – *no inap mekim*
fair (just) – *stret*
fall – *pundaun*
family – *famili*
famous – *i gat biknem*
fan – *brum bilong winim pes*
far – *longwe*
farmer – *man bilong wokim gaden*
fast – *kwik*
fasten – *pasim*
festival – *singsing*
fetch – *kisim ... i kam*
few – *wan wan* or *lik lik*
field – *ples kunai*
fight (vb) – *pait*
fill – *pulapim*
film (camera) – *pilum*
film (movie show) – *piksa*
finally – *pinis tru*

find – *painim pinis*
finish – *pinisim*
fire – *paia*
first – *namba wan*
fish (n) – *pis*
flat – *stret*
flat (tyre) – *taia i plat*
floor – *purpur*
flower – *plaua*
fly (n) – *langa*
fly (vb) – *flai*
follow – *bihainim*
food – *kaikai*
foot – *fut*
football – *kikbal*
for – *long*
forbidden – *i tambu*
foreign – *bilong longwe ples*
forest – *bus*
forget – *lusim tingting*
fork – *pok*
former – *bipo*
forwards – *poret*
free (vacant) – *i no gat man o meri*
fresh – *nupela*
fried – *i bin praim*
fried rice – *prairais*
friend – *pren*
from – *long*
front of, in – *ai bilong*
frontier – *arere bilong kantri*
frozen – *i ais pinis*

fruit – *pikinini bilong diwai*
full – *pulap*

G

garden – *gaden*
gasoline – *bensin*
girl – *meri*
give – *givim*
glad – *hamamas*
glass (container) – *glas*
glass (substance) – *glas*
glove – *soken bilong han*
go – *go*
go down – *go daun*
go up – *go antap*
god – *god*
gold – *gol*
good – *gutpela*
goods – *kago*
government – *gavman*
gram – *giram*
grapes – *ol pikinini bilong rop wain*
grass – *gras*
green – *grin*
grey – *gre*
ground – *graun* or *giraun*
guard (vb) – *sambai long*
guest – *pasindia*
guide – *man i soim rot* or *gait*
guidebook – *buk em i soim rot*
gun – *gan*

H

hair – *gras bilong het*
haircut – *katim gras*
hairdresser – *man i save katim gras bilong het*
ham – *lek bilong pik*
handbag – *hanpaus*
handkerchief – *kankisip*
harbour (n) – *pasis*
hard – *hatpela* or *strongpela*
hat – *hat*
have – *gat*
he – *em*
head – *het*
headache – *het i pen*
hear – *harim*
heart – *kilok*
heavy – *hevi*
height – *longpela bilong en*
help (vb) – *halivim*
her – *bilong em*
here – *hia*
high – *antap*
hill – *maunten*
his – *bilong em*
hold – *holim*
holy – *tambu*
home, at – *long haus*
honest – *stret*
hope – *hop*
horse – *hos*
hospital – *haus sik*
host – *bos bilong haus*

hot – *hat*
hot season (summer) – *taim bilong san*
hotel – *hotel*
hour – *aua*
house (n) – *haus*
how – *olsem wanem*
how many – *hamas*
however – *tasol*
hut – *haus*

I

I – *mi*
ice – *ais*
ice cream – *aiskrim*
if – *sapos*
ill – *sik*
immediately – *stret nau*
important – *i bikpela samting*
impossible – *i hat moa*
in – *insait long*
information – *toksave*
inside – *insait*
instead of – *long halivim*
interesting – *i laikim tru*
interpreter – *man i tanim tok ples*
iron (metal) – *ain*
is – *stap*
island – *ailan*
isn't it? – *laka?*
it – *em*

J

Jewellery – *bilas*
Journey – *wokabaut*
Jump (vb) – *kalap*
Jungle – *bus*

K

Kill – *kilim i dai pinis*
Kilogram – *kilogiram*
Kilometre – *kilomita*
Kind (friendly) – *gut*
King – *king*
Kiss (vb) – *givim kis*
Kitchen – *haus kuk*
Knife – *naip*
Know (vb) – *save*

L

Label – *namba*
Lake – *raunwara*
Lamb – *pikinini bilong sipsip*
Last – *bihain tru*
Late (behind time) – *bihaintaim* or *taim i lus*
Later – *bai* or *bihain*
Laugh – *lap*
Laundry (clothes) – *klos was*
Law – *lo*
Lawyer – *loman*
Lead (vb) – *go pas long*
Learn – *lainim*
Least, at – *liklik tru*
Leave (place) – *lusim*

leave behind – *larim*
left (hand) – *lep*
leg – *lek*
lemon – *muli*
lemonade – *loliwara*
letter (note) – *pas*
letter (character) – *rait*
lettuce – *letis*
lie (n) – *giaman*
lie down – *slip*
lift (vb) – *liptimupim*
light (colour) – *tulait*
light (weight) – *i no hevi*
lighter (cigarette) – *sigaret laita*
like – *olsem long*
lipstick – *pen bilong maus*
litre – *lita*
little, a – *liklik*
live (reside) – *stap*
lock (n) – *lok*
long (size) – *longpela*
long (time) – *longpela taim*
long ago – *bipo tru*
look at – *lukim*
look for – *painim*
lose (mislay) – *lusim*
loud – *strong*
love – *laikim*
low – *daun*
lunch – *liklik kaikai* or *belo*

M

machine (n) – *masin*
magazine – *niuspepa*
make – *wokim*
malaria – *malaria*
man – *man*
manager – *menaga*
mango – *mango*
many – *planti*
map – *map*
market – *bung*
married – *i marit*
matches – *masis*
means, (it) – *i min*
measure (vb) – *makim*
meat – *abus*
mechanic – *mekanik*
medicine – *marasin*
meet – *painim*
melon – *melen*
menu – *pas bilong ol kaikai*
message – *tok*
metre – *mita*
middle – *namel*
midnight – *biknait*
milk (n) – *susu*
millimetre – *milimita*
minute – *minit*
mirror – *glas bilong lukluk*
mistake – *i no stret*
moment – *minit*
monastery – *haus pater*

money – *mani*
month – *mun*
monument – *makim*
moon – *mun*
more – *moa*
morning – *moningtaim*
mosque – *haus lotu bilong ol mahomet*
mosquito – *natnat*
most – *moa tru*
motor-bike – *motobaik*
mountain – *maunten*
mouth – *maus*
movie camera – *kamera piksa*
much – *planti*
museum – *haus bilong tumbuna pasin*
mushroom – *papai*
music – *musik* or *sing sing*
must – *mas*
mustard – *mastet*
my – ... *bilong mi*

N

name (n) – *nem*
napkin – *napkin*
narrow – *i no brait*
natural – *samting tru*
near (not far) – *klostu*
near to – *klostu long*
need – *laikim*
needle (n) – *nil bilong samap*
never – *i no gat wanpela taim*
new – *nupela*

newspaper – *niuspepa*
next (after) – *bihain*
night – *nait*
no – *nogat*
nobody – *i no gat man*
noise – *nois*
noodles – *ol nudal*
noon – *belo kaikai*
north – *not*
not – *no*
not at all – *no ... tasol*
notepaper – *pepa bilong raitim leta*
nothing – *i no gat samting*
notice – *toksave*
now – *nau*
number – *namba*
nurse (n) – *nes*
nuts – *galip*

O

obtain – *kisim*
occupied – *pulap*
offer – *mekim ofa*
office – *ofis*
officer (army) – *ofisa*
often – *planti taim*
oil – *wel*
old (persons) – *lapun*
old (things) – *olpela*
olives – *pikinini diwai oliv*
on – *antap long*
once – *wanpela taim*

onion – *anian*
only – *tasol*
open – *i op i stap*
open (vb) – *opim*
opera – *kain singsing na danis*
opposite – *arasait*
or – *no*
orange – *switmuli*
ordered – *takim*
ordinary – *nating*
our – *bilong mipela*
outside – *ausait*
overcoat – *kotren*
owe – *gat dinau*
oyster – *kina*

P

pack (vb) – *bungim wantaim*
pain – *pen*
paint (n) – *pen*
pair – *tupela*
palace – *haus bilong king*
paper – *pepa*
parcel – *karamap*
park (n) – *gaden bilas*
park (car) (vb) – *pasim kar*
passport – *paspot*
pastry – *kek*
pay (vb) – *peim*
peace – *gutpela taim*
pearl – *kiau bilong golip*
peas – *hebsen*

pen – *pen*
pencil – *pensil*
pepper – *pepa*
perfume – *sanda*
perhaps – *nating*
permit (vb) – *larim*
person – *man o meri*
petrol (gasoline) – *bensin*
pharmacy – *haus marasin*
photograph (n) – *poto*
picture (n) – *piksa*
piece – *hap*
pillow – *pilo*
pin – *pin*
pineapple – *painup*
pink – *ret*
place – *hap*
plate (n) – *plet*
platform (railway) – *ples bilong wetim tren*
pleasant – *switpela*
point out – *mekim long pinga long*
police station – *polis stesin*
policeman – *polisman*
poor (needy) – *nogat moni*
pork – *abus pik*
porter – *kagoboi*
possible – *i ken*
post-box – *letabokis*
postcard – *poskat*
post-office – *haus pos*
potatoes – *poteto*
practise – *traim*

prawn – *kindam bilong solwara* or *liklik kindam*
preacher – *talatala*
present (gift) – *presen*
president – *presiden*
press (clothes) – *ainim*
pretty – *nais*
price – *pe*
priest – *pater*
prison – *kalabus*
private – *tambu long olgeta*
promise – *promisim*
public – *bilong olgeta man na meri*
pull – *pulim ... i kam*
puncture – *taia i plat*
pure – *klin*
purple – *hap ret*
put – *putim*

Q

quantity – *hamas*
queen – *misis kwin*
question – *kwestin*
quick – *hariap*
quiet – *i no gat nois* or *no ken mekim nois*

R

race (contest) – *resis*
radio – *wailis*
railway – *tren*
raincoat – *kotren*
raining, it is – *ren i kamdaun* or *ren i pundaun*
rather – *liklik*

razor – *resa*
read – *ritim*
ready – *redi*
receive – *kisim*
record (gramophone) – *rekot*
red – *ret*
register (letter) – *rejistarim pas*
religion – *lotu*
remember – *holim long tingting* or *no lusim tingting*
repair (vb) – *wokim gut*
repeat – *mekim gen*
reply – *bekim tok*
rest – *malolo*
restaurant – *haus kaikai*
result – *ansa*
rice (cooked) – *rais*
rich – *i gat planti samting*
right (correct) – *stret*
right (hand) – *han sut*
ring (n) – *ring*
ripe – *mau*
river – *wara*
road – *rot*
roast – *i bin kukim long paia*
room (n) – *rum*
run – *ran*

S

sad – *i sori*
safe – *i stap gut*
sailor – *boskru*
salt – *sol*

same – *wankain*
sandals – *sandal*
sandwich – *sanwis*
sauce – *sos*
say – *tokim*
school – *skul*
science – *save*
scissors – *sisis*
sea – *solwara*
seat – *sia*
second – *namba tu*
second (time) – *sekon*
secretary – *kuskus*
see – *lukim*
seems – *ating*
seldom – *sampela taim*
sell – *salim*
send (thing) – *salim*
servant – *hausboi*
service station – *sevis stesin*
several – *sampela*
sew – *samapim*
shallow – *i no daun*
shampoo – *sop*
shave – *sepim*
she – *em*
sheet – *bet laplap* or *bet sit*
shelter (n) – *ples bilong hait*
ship (n) – *sip*
shirt – *siot*
shoe – *su*
shop (n) – *stua*

short – *sot*
show (vb) – *soim*
shower (n) – *waswas*
side – *hapsait*
sign (vb) – *raitim nem long*
silk – *slika*
silver – *silva*
since (time) – *bihain long*
sing – *singsing*
sit – *sindaun*
skirt – *siket*
sky – *heven*
sleep – *slip*
slow – *slo*
small – *liklik*
smoke (vb) – *smok* or *simuk*
snow – *ais*
soap – *sop*
socks – *sokin*
soda water – *sodawara*
soft – ... *malmalum*
soldier – *soldia*
some – *sampela*
somebody – *wanpela man no meri*
something – *wanpela samting*
sometimes – *sampela taim*
somewhere – *long sampela hap*
soon – *kwiktaim*
sorry – *sore*
soup – *sup*
sour – *soua*
south – *saut*

soy sauce – *soi sos*
space – *spes*
speak – *tokim*
spectacles – *aiglas*
spoon – *spun*
sport – *pilai*
stairs – *leta*
stamp (postage) – *stem*
stand – *sanap*
star – *sta*
start – *kirapim*
station (railway) – *tren stesin*
stay – *sindaun* or *stap*
steak – *mit*
steep – *i go daun tumas*
steering – *stia*
still (adv) – *yet*
stockings – *sokin*
stone – *ston*
storey (floor) – *plo*
straight on – *stret*
strap – *pasim*
street – *rot*
string – *string*
strong – *strongpela*
student – *studen* or *sumatin*
study (vb) – *lainim*
substance – *samting*
suddenly – *santu*
sugar – *suga*
suitcase – *paus*
summit – *antap*

sun – *san*
sweet – *swit*
swim – *swim*

T

table (n) – *tebol*
tailor (n) – *man bilong samapim klos*
take – *kisim*
tall – *long*
tape (recording) – *tep*
tape recorder – *teprikoda*
taste (vb) – *traiim*
tax (n) – *takis*
taxi – *taksi*
tea – *ti*
teach – *skulim*
teacher – *tisa*
telegram – *wailis*
telephone – *telipon*
television – *bokis wailis wantem piksa*
temperature – *makim hat o kol*
temple – *haus lotu*
than – *long*
that – *dispela*
theatre – *haus piksa*
their – *bilong ol*
then (at that time) – *dispela taim*
there – *long hap*
there is – *i gat*
they – *ol*
thick – *strong*
thin – *bun nating*

thing – *samting*
think – *tingting*
third – *namba tri*
thirsty – *hangre long dring*
this – *dispela*
thread (n) – *tret*
through – *long namel long*
throw – *tromoi*
ticket – *tiket*
ticket-office – *tiket ofis*
tie (n) – *nektait*
time – *taim*
timetable – *taimtebol*
tin opener – *op tin*
tired – *i les*
to – *long*
tobacco – *tabak*
today – *tude*
together – *wantaim*
toilet (men) – *haus pekpek man*
toilet (women) – *haus pekpek meri*
toilet paper – *pepa pekpek*
tomato – *tomato*
tomorrow – *tumora*
tonight – *tunait*
too – *tumas*
toothbrush – *bros bilong tit*
toothpaste – *sop bilong tit*
touch – *pilim*
tourist – *kam man*
towards – *long hap i go long*
towel – *taul*

tower – *taua*
town – *taun*
town hall – *kaunsel haus*
train – *tren*
translate – *tanim tok ples*
travel – *wokabaut*
tree – *diwai*
trouble – *trabel*
trousers – *trausis*
true – *tru*
try on – *traim*
twice – *tupela taim*
typewriter – *taipraita*
typist – *taipis*
tyre – *taia*

U

ugly – *i no naispela*
umbrella – *ambrela*
under – *ananit long*
understand – *save*
unfortunately – *tarangu*
university – *univesiti*
until – *inap long*
upstairs – *antap*
urgently – *kwiktaim*
usually – *save*

V

valley – *ples daun*
valuable – *i kastim planti mani*
veal – *mit bilong pikinini bulmakau*

vegetables – *saior*
very – *tumas*
view (outlook) – *ples lukluk*
village – *ples*
visit – *go lukim*
voyage (n) – *wokabaut long sip*

W

wait for – *wetim*
waiter – *weta*
walk (vb) – *wokabaut*
wall – *banis*
want – *laik*
war – *pait*
wash (vb) – *wasim*
washbasin – *dis bilong waswas*
watch (n) – *hanwas*
water – *wara*
we – *mipela*
weather (n) – *taim*
week – *wik*
weight – *skel*
well (adv) – *gut*
well (health) – *i stap gut*
west – *wes*
wet – *i gat wara*
wet season – *taim bilong ren*
wharf – *bris*
what – *wanem samting*
wheel – *wil*
when – *wataim* or *wanem taim*
where – *we*

which – *wanem*
white – *wait*
who – *husat*
whose – *bilong husat*
why – *bilong wanem*
wide – *brait*
wild – *wail*
win – *winim*
wind (n) – *win*
window – *windo*
wine – *wain*
wise – *i save tumas*
with – *wantaim*
without – *i no gat*
woman – *meri*
wonder – *tingim . . . o nogat*
wonderful – *nais tumas*
wood (timber) – *diwai*
wool – *gras bilong sipsip*
word – *tok*
work – *wok*
workman – *wokman*
world – *graun*
worse – *moa nogut*
worst – *nambawan nogut*
worth – *kastim*
write – *raitim*
wrong – *kranki*

Y

year – *yia*
yellow – *yelo*

yesterday – *asde*
you – *yu*
young – *yang*
your – *bilong yu*